# RASPUTIN: The Mysterious Monk

by
Janet Serlin Garber

Illustrated
by
Heidi Schmeck

cpi
contemporary perspectives, inc.

This book is distributed by Silver Burdett Company, Morristown, New Jersey 07960.

Library of Congress Number: 78-24348

Art and Photo Credits

**Cover illustration by Heidi Schmeck.**
Photos on pages 15, 17, 21, 23, 25, and 33, Culver Pictures, Inc.
Photos on pages 27, 29, and 37, Photoworld.
Photo on page 35, Beinecke Rare Book and Manuscript Library, Yale University.
Every effort has been made to trace the ownership of all copyrighted material in this
book and to obtain permission for its use.

**Library of Congress Cataloging Publication Data**

Garber, Janet Serlin.
  Rasputin: the mysterious monk

  SUMMARY: Recounts the life of Rasputin, the
controversial figure who so influenced the Russian court
of Nicholas and Alexandra that he brought about his own
assassination.
  1. Rasputin, Grigoríí Efimovich, 1871-1916 —
Juvenile literature. 2. Russia — Court and courtiers —
Biography — Juvenile literature. 3. Russia — History
— Nicholas II, 1894-1917 — Juvenile literature. [1.
Rasputin, Grigoríí Efimovich, 1871-1916. 2. Russia —
History — Nicholas II; 1894-1917 — Biography] I. Title.
DK254.R3G37   947.08′092′4 [B]   78-24348
ISBN 0-89547-072-1

Manufactured in the United States of America
ISBN 0-89547-072-1

# Contents

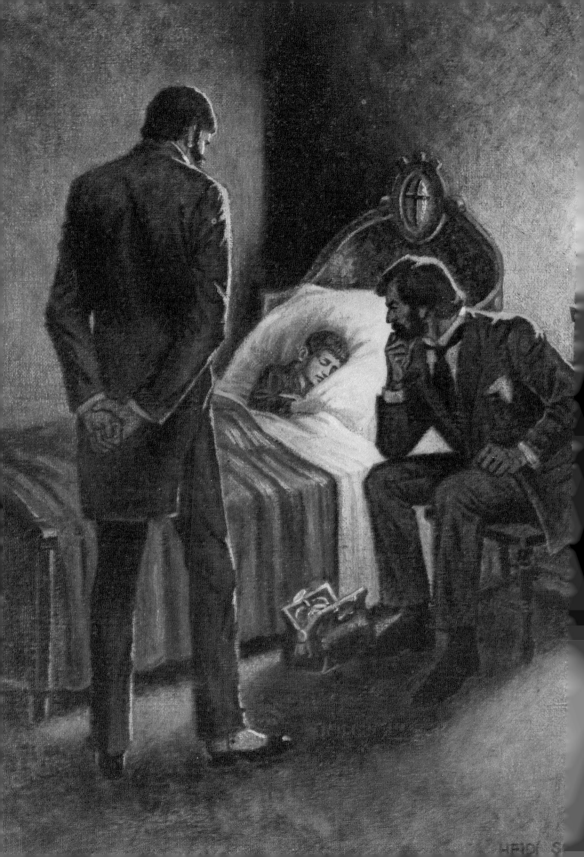

# Chapter 1

# The Magic Cure

The curtains were drawn. Only candle flames lighted the dim room. A large bed stood against one wall. Almost hidden under the blankets was the tiny outline of a small boy. Alexis Nicholaievitch Romanov lay very still.

Alexis, who was only four years old, was very sick. His worried family and doctors circled his bed. The doctors had done all they could. Now all they could do was wait and hope. They stood and sadly shook their heads. Only a miracle could save the boy, and no miracle was in sight.

The year was 1908, and doctors still knew little about the young boy's illness. They did know that

Alexis had been born with hemophilia, or "the bleeders' disease." The blood of a person with hemophilia does not *clot*, or thicken, as it should. Because of this, every small cut and bruise was a danger for Alexis. The smallest accident caused him to bleed.

Alexis was a prince, the son of Tsar Nicholas and Tsarina Alexandra of Russia. As their oldest son, he was next in line to the throne. But right now that did not matter to his unhappy family. At this terrible time, Alexis was just their son and they loved him very much.

"Can nothing be done?" the Tsarina sadly asked the doctors. They stood by the bed in silence. "We have tried everything," they finally said, as the worried mother walked back and forth across the room.

"I shall have prayers said for him all over the palace! All over St. Petersburg!" she cried. But the prayers did not seem to help Alexis. For three days he lay in bed bleeding.

Alexis's attack began one day while he was playing with his friends. While running, he tripped and fell. He got up and went on playing. But later that night he felt a pain in his leg and told his mother. He was put right to bed but his legs had begun to swell. A few little bruises had started the bleeding inside the boy's body.

One day during this time the Grand Duchess
Olga, Alexis's aunt, came to see him. She, too,
stood sadly by the bed with the others. Suddenly she
came up with an interesting suggestion.

"You have given these doctors every chance to help
the boy, no?" she asked Alexandra. "Now you must try
something else. There is a certain holy man I have
heard about. He has worked miracles with the sick. I
shall ask him to come to the palace right away!"

And so she did. Olga sent friends to find the
mysterious holy man — a monk by the name of
Rasputin.

In a short time Rasputin was at the palace. He
rushed through a side door and past the royal guards
who stood at attention. He ran through the golden
halls and up the marble staircase.

When he entered the boy's room all eyes turned to
him. What a strange sight he was! He had a long, dirty
beard and wore rough peasant clothes. He stood out
from the richly clothed members of the royal family.
But the strangest thing about him was his eyes! They
were a very bright blue which shone like steel and
some said had great powers. With those eyes he could
place people in a deep sleep from which, it was said,
only Rasputin could awaken them.

The monk marched across the room and greeted the Tsar and Tsarina with a warm hug. He gave each of the royal couple three kisses on the cheeks — a very strange greeting from a peasant to a king and queen! Then he stood at the foot of the bed where Alexis lay in great pain. He began to pray. A sudden quiet came over the room. Rasputin stood up and began to speak softly to the prince. "Open your eyes, my son. Open your eyes and look at me."

As if by magic, Alexis's eyes fluttered and opened. He looked puzzled for a moment. Then he saw the bearded face of Rasputin. A smile slowly appeared on his little face.

"Ah, my child!" cried the Tsarina with joy. The silence was broken and the others joined in the Tsarina's cries of happiness. Rasputin raised his hand to order silence. "Your pain is going away," he said to Alexis. "You will soon be well. You must thank God for saving you. Now you will go to sleep."

Again, as if by magic, Alexis fell into a quiet sleep. There was a gentle smile on his face, the first in several days. Rasputin moved away from the bed. "Alexis, the Tsarevitch, will live," he said to the surprised people around the room. Then he turned and left.

No one who was there that evening would ever forget Rasputin's "magical" cure of the young prince.

8

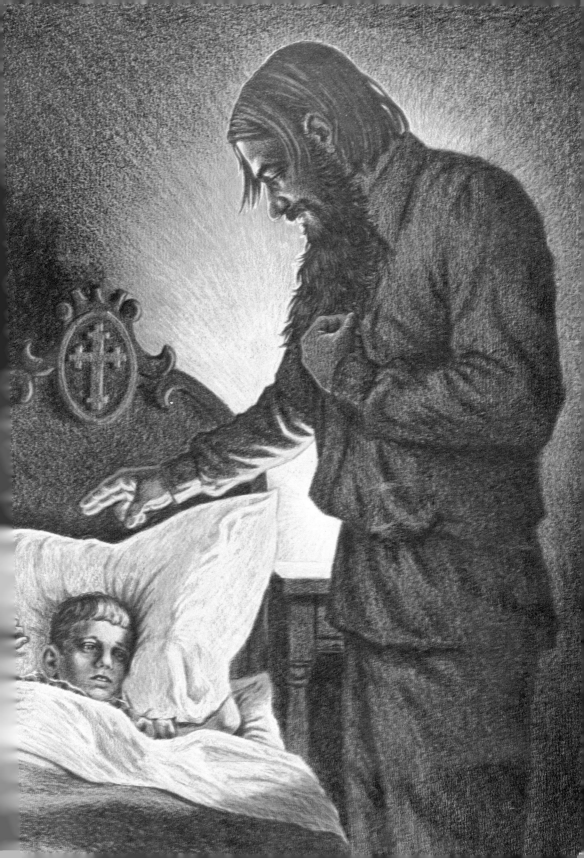

Soon Rasputin became a well-known visitor at the palace, and a lasting friendship began between Rasputin and the royal family.

But while the royal family was overjoyed and thankful to Rasputin, the royal doctors were stunned. How had Rasputin done it? How could a simple peasant stop the prince's bleeding when no doctor could? Who was this mysterious monk who seemed to heal the sick with his eyes?

In all the years since that night, people the world over have tried to solve the mystery of that man called Rasputin. But there always seem to be two sides to Rasputin's story — the one told by his enemies and the one told by his friends. He had as many of one as the other. To his friends and admirers, Rasputin was a man gifted with magical powers. To his enemies, he was an evil fake.

Whichever he was, the strange story of Rasputin's life has given the world one of the greatest unsolved mysteries of all time.

# Chapter 2

# Madman or Magician?

Very little is known about Grigori Efimovitch Rasputin. He was born in a lonely part of Siberia, that part of eastern Russia that lies north of China.

According to his daughter, who in 1977 was living in Los Angeles, California, Rasputin was born on the night of January 23, 1871. On the very same night a great meteor, or "shooting star," burned up in the sky just above the little village. The meteor was seen by many of the villagers as a sign that something of great importance was happening.

Rasputin's father and mother were very poor peasant farmers who could not read or write. Rasputin did not learn to read and write until he was a grown man. But even as a child, he claimed to have strange "visions," and he seemed able to cure farm animals that no one else could help. People in his village said that when Rasputin was near the farm animals, they seemed to work harder.

A story was told of Rasputin when he was still a small boy. He was sick in bed, listening to his father's friends talking about some horses that had been stolen. All at once the sick child sat up, looked at one of his father's friends, and shouted at the man: "You are the thief!"

Young Rasputin was beaten by his father for saying such a thing to a friend. Later that night, however, men from the village came pounding on the door of the Rasputin home. They had followed that same man and watched him steal a neighbor's horse. Young Grigori had been right! But how could he have known?

Perhaps the strangest thing about Rasputin was that he seemed to know about things before they happened. For no reason at all he would say "A stranger is coming." And sure enough, some stranger would soon appear in their tiny village that almost no one visited. This made people believe that he had "magical" powers even as a young boy.

As he grew up, Grigori Rasputin worked on his father's farm, but he led anything but a "holy" life. His friends were not the hard-working farmers of his village, but those whose actions had brought shame and disgrace upon their families. Yet there would come a day when Grigori, in his 20s, would be called a "holy man" by the greatest leaders of the Russian church. They would say that Rasputin was sent to them as a gift from heaven. If we can believe

the story Rasputin himself told, the holy men may have been right.

One day, while plowing, Rasputin had a vision. It told him, he said, to take a long trip. His father laughed at the idea and said, "Grigori has visions out of laziness!" But Rasputin set out anyway and for months walked 2,000 miles to the monastery of Mount Athos in Greece.

At the end of two years he returned home. But now there was an air of mystery about him. He prayed all the time and blessed other peasants. He began to sit by their beds when they were sick. He was thought to be a very holy and religious man. He began to wander from town to town along dusty roads. His long beard and dirty clothes would be part of him for the rest of his life. Even when he became famous, people would laugh at him because of the way he looked.

But the leaders of the Russian church did not laugh. They wanted to bring more Russian peasants back to religion. Would not Rasputin, this peasant who seemed to have the gift of magic in him, be the perfect holy man to bring the peasants back to the church? Of course he would!

But the church leaders should have asked themselves one more question. Would this holy peasant want anything to do with other Russian

Rasputin married and had three children.

peasants? Or would Rasputin, a priest of the church, become mad with his new power? Would he now rather move up in the world to become the friend of the rich rather than the poor? The enemies he would soon make in St. Petersburg would answer that question.

"Rasputin is a madman, not a holy man," they would say. "He has spent most of his life with others who are mad. Now he will stop at nothing to get what he really wants — the power of the Tsar himself!"

# Chapter 3

# Rasputin Climbs the Royal Ladder

Madman or magician, Rasputin came to St. Petersburg at just the right time. St. Petersburg was then the capital of Russia. He said he was "told" to go to the city by a voice that came to him in the night. The voice said he had something very wonderful to do for others there. His enemies, of course, said that was not the real reason Rasputin went to St. Petersburg at all. They said he went there only to make himself a rich and powerful man.

In the early 1900s, when Rasputin arrived in St. Petersburg, the well-to-do people of that large city were finding it great fun to listen to stories of magic and supernatural beings. Rasputin, the man who heard mysterious voices, the man who could heal the sick with his eyes, soon became very popular in St. Petersburg. Rich and important Russians, who never would have been friendly with someone so poor, found

16

him entertaining. This was a piece of luck for Rasputin. Through these people he would soon meet and gain the complete trust of the royal family.

Who could ever have imagined that the peasant Rasputin would someday be more powerful than even the richest and most noble Russians?

It was not long before Rasputin became a favorite of some of the most important people in St. Petersburg. He went to all the parties and balls at their grand palaces. He always greeted everyone with three kisses on the cheeks. No peasant had ever done such a thing!

Rasputin was a popular guest at parties in St. Petersburg.

A lowly Russian peasant was expected to address important people with a bow and call them "Your Excellency." But the rich people of St. Petersburg seemed to love Rasputin, even when he acted badly toward them. They said it was part of the magician's "charm."

Rasputin's fame spread quickly throughout St. Petersburg. He was more than a magician. He was known as a holy man who could see the future and change people's lives with his wise words. He was believed to use his magical eyes and hands to heal the sick whom the doctors had given up for lost. Rich and poor began to seek him out in large numbers. But as his fame grew, so did his enemies. Most were jealous of his growing power over the royal family.

And always there were more questions raised about the strange man with the long, black beard. Was Rasputin simply lucky in coming to St. Petersburg when he did? Had he really had a vision from some other world that told him this was the right time? Or had he carefully arranged things so he would meet the Tsar and Tsarina no matter what happened? Could he have known just the right moment to visit the sick prince — the very moment the bleeding would stop?

The royal family, of course, saw only the good in Rasputin. To Alexandra he was the only man who could save her son. This was the most important thing in her life. In time she would turn to Rasputin for help in *every* important matter in her life. The Tsarina was so taken with Rasputin that he was fast becoming the most important person in Russia. Through Alexandra he advised Tsar Nicholas on all problems of government. To some, Rasputin was about to become more important and more powerful than the Tsar himself.

Did Rasputin have Alexandra under some magical spell? Could he make her do anything he asked? His enemies said yes. Others, his friends, said no.

The truth was no one really knew. There was no one in Russia who was close enough to Alexandra to solve the mystery of Rasputin's power over her.

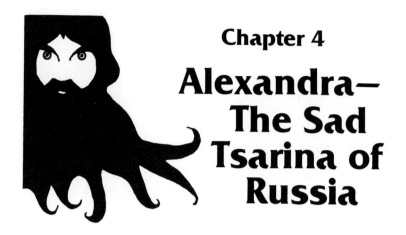

# Chapter 4

# Alexandra— The Sad Tsarina of Russia

Tsarina Alexandra was born in Germany. Her name was Princess Alix of Hesse. She came to Russia after marrying Tsar Nicholas II in 1894. As a Russian ruler, she had to take a Russian name — Alexandra Feodorovna. Alexandra was a granddaughter of the great Queen Victoria of England. It was from that bloodline that the genes with hemophilia probably came.

There was no way of knowing for certain that Alexandra's sons would be born with the disease. Of course, there was a good chance that they would, and Tsar Nicholas knew it. But the Tsar was a man in love. He married Alexandra and brought her to Russia. But the idea of this marriage was not a happy one for many of his people. Nor would they be happy with the marriage in the years to come.

In Tsarina Alexandra the Russian people saw a tall, beautiful woman, always dressed in the finest silk and

velvet gowns. Her hair was often alive with sparkling jewels and combs of gold and ivory. She was a strong but fairly quiet woman who at first appeared happy to be royal wife and mother. But slowly, her husband, Tsar Nicholas, appeared to be leaning more and more on her.

And now Alexandra seemed to have found someone strong to lean on herself. Here was someone she trusted completely. He was a holy man, who seemed to have visions that told him the future. He was Rasputin, and many Russians were afraid he was now the real ruler of their country.

Alexandra had not been very well liked by the Russian people even before Rasputin came into her life. There were those who didn't like her simply because she was not Russian. She was disliked by the rich and powerful because she kept herself apart from them. The new Tsarina was shy. She didn't make friends very easily. To make matters worse for the friendless woman, she had four daughters in a row. At a time when only a son could rule Russia, she had no boy who could follow his father to the throne.

Then, as if in answer to the sad woman's prayers, her son Alexis was born. The Tsarina was overjoyed. Alexis was looked upon as a gift from heaven. And the city of St. Petersburg was overjoyed.

But their happiness didn't last long. Six weeks later the royal parents knew the truth about their son. Alexis had hemophilia. Alexandra's heart was broken. Her dream of happiness was over and her sadness had returned. She blamed herself for her son's disease.

Alexandra now spent all her waking hours trying to keep Alexis well. She was more alone than ever.

Alexandra made a bad mistake. She and the Tsar kept

The Tsar's and Tsarina's first four children were girls.

the illness a secret from the people. No one understood
why Alexandra now spent all her time with Alexis. Of
course, she felt she needed to watch him every moment
so that he wouldn't hurt himself. The Russian people
thought that the Tsarina was just unfriendly. She was
liked less now than before Alexis was born.

How difficult it was for the poor Tsarina to simply go
to a party. She had to look happy when she was really
worried about Alexis. To all the other party guests her
sad face meant only that she didn't like them or her life
in Russia.

It was a mistake to keep Alexis's illness a secret for another reason as well. Not only did people not understand why she stayed with her son all the time, but no one understood why she spent so much time with the hated Rasputin.

Perhaps if they had known that it was Rasputin who seemed to cure Alexis, people might have hated him less. And perhaps they would have liked Alexandra more, knowing why she needed to see him so often. *Perhaps.* But even if they had liked Rasputin at the beginning, could anyone ever answer the questions that would later be asked about him?

Could anyone have believed that Rasputin was not tricking the Tsarina in order to get power for himself?

As it was, Alexandra grew more and more distant from her friends. As she did, she grew closer and closer to Rasputin. Soon only those people liked by Rasputin were asked to the palace. The Tsar's friends were very angry about this. He was no longer seen by any of them. His old friends were used to giving him advice. Now the only people talking to Tsar Nicholas were Alexandra and, of course, Rasputin. If the Tsar talked only with these two, who *was* running the country?

As for Nicholas, the Tsar could have used some good advice. He had never really liked being a ruler. His own father had often talked of passing him over and

leaving the throne to one of his younger sons. This hurt Nicholas very deeply and he never forgot it. But Nicholas had become a good Tsar in his own way and a loving husband and father. He was a kind man who spent long hours working on his official duties even when they were boring or he was tired.

By now people were not sure the Tsar was even alive. Could the evil Rasputin have cast a spell over Alexandra? Could she have plotted with him to get rid of her own husband? His friends were certain that the Tsar would never have put up with Rasputin for this long, unless the Tsar was being tricked  *Or unless Rasputin had done away with the Tsar!*

The truth that none of his friends knew was that the Tsar was as heartbroken about Alexis's illness as was his wife. As the boy grew older the attacks continued. Sometimes he had to stay in bed for long periods of time. But when he was well, he was as cheerful and active as any boy his age.

Every time Alexis had an attack it seemed like the end. The doctors were called in to do what they could, but they could never help very much. Finally, the Tsarina would call upon Rasputin. For some strange reason, he managed to stop the boy's bleeding every time.

No one has ever figured out how Rasputin's magic helped the sick child. His enemies later said he had the power to hypnotize the young prince — to put the boy under a spell  — and then heal him by working on his mind. Others would claim that Rasputin and the doctors were working together. First they made Alexis sick with small bits of poison. The poisoning would stop, they said, just before Rasputin was called in to

help. This made it appear that it was Rasputin alone who cured Alexis, as if by magic.

The Tsar saw what Alexandra saw — a sick child who became well whenever Rasputin came to him. The Tsar also heard the awful stories being told about Rasputin. Like the Tsarina, he would not listen to them. But Tsar Nicholas was no better able to explain Rasputin's magic with his son than was his wife. How could anyone explain magic such as this?

Today it is hard to accept Rasputin as a magician. Modern-day doctors offer us a better explanation for Rasputin's healing powers. Perhaps Rasputin's secret was that he had a calming effect on Alexis. This would slow the boy's heartbeat and the flow of his blood. Imagine Alexis, frightened by the pain and by the faces of his worried family. The doctors would hurry in, one after the other. Each would be nervous, too, and would only scare Alexis more.

Then Rasputin would arrive. Only his powerful manner would bring calm to the room. His deep voice would soothe the frightened child. The Tsarina's great trust in him could be felt in the air.

Rasputin would tell the boy one story after another. He would talk about peasant life, and magic, and he would tell funny fairy tales. Little Alexis would forget his pain and fear as Rasputin told his stories. The boy's heartbeat would slow. The bleeding would stop. Soon the swellings in his body would go away. Tired from his pain, the Tsarevitch would finally fall into a deep sleep.

To the worried parents in the sickroom, this bearded man certainly would seem to be a magician. But at the time no one, not even Rasputin, could have known what doctors know about hemophilia today. The patient can be helped during an attack by a calming influence. But a hemophilia attack gets worse when the patient is frightened.

28

Nicholas and Alexandra didn't care how Rasputin cured their son. All they knew was that he could work wonders where everyone else failed.

So the royal family chose to overlook all the stories about Rasputin and his wicked ways. They cared only about the health of their son. As for the Tsar, he had many other problems on his mind. There was great unrest in Russia. Groups of people were plotting to destroy the crown and do away with royalty in Russia once and for all.

The Tsar's rich friends and family were sending messages to him night and day. *The mood of the people grows worse each moment! The Tsar must send his soldiers against the peasants who want to destroy us! ... Your love of Rasputin is the reason the peasants are so unhappy with us! Yes, Rasputin, the evil peasant, controls your wife, and together they will destroy all of us!*

But the Tsar, in his trusting way, believed Rasputin was a simple, yet unusually gifted peasant. He saw in Rasputin "the soul of the Russian people."

Rasputin's enemies increased. As they did, his very life was in danger. The Tsarina had to hire secret guards to watch over him at all times.

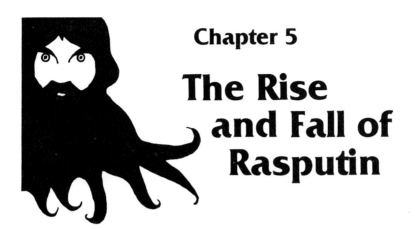

# Chapter 5

# The Rise
## and Fall of
## Rasputin

The year was 1913. Life for Tsar Nicholas was becoming a bad dream. His wife, Alexandra, would not stop defending Rasputin for a moment. The Tsar was torn between love for his wife and the hatred his family and friends had for Rasputin. And now a new problem was around the corner. Not only might he be at war with his own Russian people, but there seemed to be a great world war on the way.

Alexandra was telling her husband what to do all the time. Rasputin had told her a war would destroy the royal throne of Russia. He wanted the Tsar to have nothing to do with the war. Through Alexandra the Tsar heard of Rasputin's visions: The war would destroy the royal family once and for all. He, Rasputin, had "seen" it, the Tsarina told Nicholas.

By 1914 England and France were at war with Germany and Austria. World War I had begun. The

Tsar, now ruled almost completely by Rasputin's visions and Alexandra's pleas, tried to keep Russia out of the war. The more his wife defended Rasputin, the more the rest of the Tsar's family warned him: "Rasputin is evil. Listen to him no more. He rules Alexandra's mind and now she is ruling *your* mind!"

The Tsar tried every way open to him to keep Russia from joining the war against Germany. He knew that if she stayed out of the war, Russia could never again count on friendship and help from Britain, France, or the United States. Over and over again he read a letter he had received from Rasputin — a letter of warning.

In his letter to the Tsar, Rasputin warned that Russia would never again have a Tsar if the country were now to fight a war. The royal family would be destroyed and the poor people of Russia would rise up to take over the government. He *knew* this to be what would happen. And Tsar Nicholas believed him.

In the end, however, there was no way for Russia to stay out of the war. The Tsar not only had to join the fight against Germany, he also decided to lead his four and a half million Russian soldiers as their general. Nicholas left St. Petersburg to go to the front lines of battle. He was sure his armies would quickly move through Poland and Germany to strike at the very heart of the enemy's capital city, Berlin.

Rasputin even tried to influence Russia's military leaders.

Left at home to go on leading the Russian people was his beloved wife, Alexandra. To help the Tsarina, Nicholas knew, there would always be one person — the mighty *Rasputin*.

At first things went well with the war. The Tsar's armies fought bravely. But many thousands of Russian soldiers were needlessly lost as Nicholas ordered them to move more quickly than they should have. Even though he was far from home, he received daily letters from Alexandra with ideas about what to do in the war. She always carefully worded her advice, saying no more than she "thought" something should be done, or "wished" it would be done. The Tsar gave in easily to her suggestions. After all, had they not come from Rasputin himself?

In St. Petersburg, people now spoke openly against the Tsar. It was bad enough that Alexandra was leading the army through her husband. What was worse was that she was under the power of Rasputin. He now told her what to do in all matters. All good jobs in the government went to friends of Alexandra's and Rasputin's. Soon it seemed that they were the only ones who could grant *any* jobs in Russia. Fighting a war, the Tsar could not pay much attention to the people's anger.

It was becoming clear to Rasputin that he now had terrible enemies in two camps. The peasants who wanted to destroy the royal family hated him as much as rich and powerful people of St. Petersburg did. The Tsar's own relatives were also angered by Rasputin's hold over the Tsar and Tsarina. As long as there was a Rasputin, they would have no power at all over the Tsar.

Tsar Nicholas and his officers join Russian troops during World War I.

# Chapter 6

# Kill the "Holy Man"!

Many people are sure that Rasputin knew he would soon be killed. In 1916 he wrote a letter to the Tsar that no one to this day can explain.

*I feel that I shall leave life before January 1. If I am killed by my brothers, the Russian peasants, you, Tsar of Russia, have nothing to fear. But if it is your relatives ... then none of your children or relations will remain alive for more than two years. They will be killed by the Russian people.*

Could Rasputin really have known that, even as he wrote, the Tsar's relatives were planning to kill him? Was it just a feeling because Rasputin knew he had so many enemies? Or was it another of the visions that had made him so famous?

Behind the plan to kill Rasputin was Prince Felix Youssoupov — one of the richest men in Russia. Youssoupov's wife was the cousin of Tsarina Alexandra.

Prince Youssoupov and his wife plotted to kill Rasputin.

The prince easily found five friends to go along with his murder plan.

On the night of December 29, 1916, Rasputin went alone to Prince Youssoupov's palace. The prince had invited Rasputin to have tea and cakes with him and his wife. Rasputin worried about going there alone late at night. He probably went just to meet the princess. She was said to be one of the most beautiful women in St. Petersburg.

When Rasputin got to the palace, Youssoupov led him downstairs to a large comfortable room. The two men sat in soft chairs next to a roaring fire. Youssoupov put some of Rasputin's favorite dancing songs on a fancy record player. His wife, Youssoupov told Rasputin, was upstairs and would join them shortly.

They chatted like old friends for a while and Youssoupov passed Rasputin a plate of cakes. What Rasputin didn't know was that each cake had enough poison to kill several men instantly. While Youssoupov waited for him to fall over, Rasputin licked his lips, ate another cake and asked for a glass of wine.

His hands shaking, Youssoupov poured Rasputin a glass of wine. The wine had enough poison in it to kill a mule. Rasputin took the glass with a smile and gulped it down. He asked for another. Then he got up and danced merrily to the music.

Youssoupov's friends waited upstairs. All were frightened now as they heard Rasputin humming and dancing on the floor below. For a "dead" man, Rasputin was having a wonderful time. Finally, Youssoupov could stand it no longer. He ran upstairs

to ask his friends to help throw Rasputin out of the house. The prince had given up trying to kill the magical Rasputin.

"Igor," he whispered to his friend, "what am I to do? That devil is in there having a fine time. He is hurt by nothing. I cannot stand to watch him a moment longer. Get him out of my house!"

Youssoupov's friend Igor shook him. "Felix, you fool! We cannot let him leave here. He will only die in the street. Everyone knows he has been to your house tonight. No, you must go back downstairs before he wonders what's going on. And take this." He pressed a tiny golden gun into Youssoupov's hand.

Youssoupov came back downstairs. All was quiet. Was Rasputin dead at last? The prince opened the door. There was Rasputin, standing in front of the fire. Without a word, Youssoupov drew his gun and fired. Rasputin screamed and fell to the floor. Youssoupov, wet and shaking, slumped into a chair. Finally, it was over.

But suddenly the murderer heard a noise that sent chills through his whole body. He looked up to see the icy blue eyes of Rasputin looking at him with pure hatred. The "dead" man got to his feet. Youssoupov was so terrified that he turned and ran from the room. Rasputin stumbled up the stairs after him, growling in pain and rage.

Youssoupov ran past his friends, yelling, "Shoot him! He's still alive!" But the others were too frightened to move.

Rasputin had known, almost from the very moment he came to this house, that something was wrong. Youssoupov had seemed frightened. His hands had shaken all through the evening. Rasputin now knew why. The princess was not even home! He had been tricked by an enemy who had just tried to kill him.

His body filled with deadly poison, a bullet burning somewhere within him, Rasputin reached the top of the steps.

Finally, one of Youssoupov's friends pulled himself together and ran after Rasputin. In the courtyard he shot at Rasputin three times. At last Rasputin fell to the snow-covered ground. Quickly, the murderers tied up the body and carried it to a hole they had cut in the frozen Neva River. They pushed the body down through the hole into the ice-cold water below.

When the body was found it was learned that Rasputin had not died of the huge amount of poison he had eaten nor the gunshot wounds he had received. After all that, Rasputin was still alive when he was pushed into the Neva River. Rasputin died from drowning.

# Chapter 7

# A Voice from the Grave

After Rasputin's death things went very badly for Tsar Nicholas and his family. The war had turned on the Tsar. Two million Russian soldiers had been killed. And now Nicholas sent his family — his wife Alexandra, their son Alexis, their four daughters — from St. Petersburg to their country house. Had Rasputin not warned him that his family would be killed by the Russian people who would overthrow the government? Perhaps they would be safe in the country.

When Rasputin had been dead about three months, Tsar Nicholas left his family to join his troops. As his train neared St. Petersburg the Tsar was pulled from his coach by a group of Russians trying to take over the capital and the throne. The Tsar and his family were kept prisoners, while Rasputin's coffin was dug up and thrown into a fire. All the unhappy Alexandra could think about were the words of her mysterious friend Rasputin when, years ago, he had told her: "When I

die, my body will be burned and my ashes will fly with the winds."

In 1918, after more than a year as prisoners of the new "people's government," Rasputin's final vision came true. Tsar Nicholas, Tsarina Alexandra, Tsarevitch Alexis, and his four sisters were all killed by a Russian firing squad.

Even in death Rasputin's visions were coming true. He had once told Nicholas to fear the number seven "Never try anything risky on a date that has the number seven in it," he had said. "It is an unlucky number for us." The date of the Tsar and his family's death was, mysteriously enough, July 17 — a date with two number sevens in it! (July is the seventh month of the year.)

The Russia of Rasputin's time and the Russia of today are very different. In place of the Tsar is a whole new form of government. Would the Russian Tsar ever have been overthrown if Rasputin had not had so much power over the Tsarina? Would the things that happened to the royal family have happened anyway? Would Russia have been better off without Rasputin?

Did Rasputin really follow the voices that just happened to lead him right to the royal family? Or did

he plan his life so that each step he took led him closer to where he had been headed all along?

Did Rasputin really have magical powers to cure the sick when even doctors failed? Or was he merely a good hypnotist who put people in trances so they had no choice but to obey his will?

Was he really guided by visions to be a leader of the Russian people? Or was he just a clever man who found a way to do this by tricky means?

Did Rasputin have special powers that showed him pictures of the future? Were these pictures just lucky guesses? Or did he arrange events so that they happened to fit his pictures?

Was Rasputin a magician or a madman? Whatever you decide, you'll find many who agree with you . . . and just as many who don't.